2022 Copyright (c) Joseph E L Baruwa BSc DipBSOM All rights reserved

Printed and self published in the United Kingdom

This book may not be recreated or reproduced in written or, electronic, mechanical or any other form, by any means without permission of the writer.

Cover art and all written work, produced and published By Joseph E L Baruwa BSc DipBSOM
Meditation teacher
#MOTDLife.

You are the light
The wonder and the mystery
Let your soulfire ignite and your passions play out in the now
Unfold into and of love gracefully
With infinite illuminations of life

For my Son and Family

FORWARD

In 2021 I published a book called 'MOTD journal', which is a unique collection of 'messages of the day' and a journal for the reader. The book was written with the ambition to encourage the reader to begin a daily writing practice, to get in touch with their inner self and cultivate their own unique wisdom. The book also introduced the reader to breathing practices and meditation. After starting meditation as a regular morning ritual in 2019, I began focusing on my creativity and strengthening my practice by attending two online meditation and journaling courses. I then took on a teaching diploma with the British School of Meditation receiving a distinction to teach meditation in 2021. I truly believe that my daily writing practice and meditation go hand in hand and are an evolution of my personal purpose and style as a philosophical writer and poet. This has encouraged me to go deep within my practice and following each meditation and journaling I have collated a series of poems and meditations directly from within. I write something new every day and have done since 2010. I have self published five poetry books including 'MOTD Journal' and MOTD 'The Poetic Self' is my sixth book and second in the series of meditation compilations.

MOTD began as an acronym for Messages Of The Day and has evolved into Meditation of the Day. Just like my regular daily practices of writing a new message each day has evolved into a morning yogasana practice, energy healing and meditation followed by journaling that is now the beginnings of my daily poetry writing practice.

The Poetic Self is a collection of poetry and reflections following my morning ritual of yoga and meditation. Meditation is known to enhance creativity and can unlock intuitive thought connecting you with your highest authentic self. This book is something I would hope helps guide my son in his future years as a young man and, I would like to believe that each piece has a profound message for any reader. I believe these pages are firstly my unique interpretation of enlightenment and a reflection of inward philosophical seeking through poetry and meditation, but secondly and equally as important a compilation of poetic spiritual guidance.

CONTENT

- Self Recognises Self
- The Light
- You are...
- Solo Blooming
- As Love
- A Message of the Day
- Fatherhood
- Being the Witness
- The Sun
- Spirit Animal Search
- Blindingly Jazzing the Rays
- Weightless in Freedom
- Layers of Consciousness
- Karma
- Be Still
- Breathe and Flow
- Dimensional
- Being of Oneness
- Path Building on Abundance
- Live Through Your Gifts
- Parallel Lines
- Poetry and the Self
- Prosper in Your Greatness
- Go Within
- Kindness is Key
- Being Free
- In Peace

PEACE

- Posture
- Meditation of the Day
- Elevate
- Your Story
- Tuning into Life Force
- Walking with Kindness

ABUNDANCE

- Being of gratitude
- Creativity and Grace
- The Art of Will
- Clearing
- Divinity Unseen
- Reflections of Bliss
- Infinite Journeying
- For Jericho
- Everything You Do
- Synchronicity
- There is Only Now in The Message
- Being the Work of The Present

Self Recognises Self

It is,
With the wonderment of awareness and,
The acknowledgement of the self
Knowing you are infinite in the endless moment of now,
That will awaken you from seeking enlightenment,
To being the enlightenment.

The Light

There are changes through this life that feel like time is altering you, yet time is but the construct of opportunity for you to shine your light.
To shine on shadows that fell deep in sleep at youth and, dream travelled beneath the veil, somewhat in the universes unknown, now sat adjacent to your inner child.
Changes that show you that everything is consciousness and,
Even I derived in consciousness, before these words were birthed
That something about the self is more and must become one with the light
That inward is the way to self and solve, to heal and see
That I am, in consciousness, everything
Checking and unfolding into the sun unto your power and purpose,
Being of love and meaning
Saving and downloading the context of the changes for better and for lesson
For the embrace,
To synchronise your whole being with the rise and fall of the moon,
Whole and one with awareness
Trusting the blanket we sleep and walk beneath
Sky diving through risks on dreams, courageously through the unconditioning
Hopeful with faith, releasing with grace
For time as we are taught is forward and, unfolds the untold beauty of the shadow within
Yet the same is told with stillness and breath,
Deeper and freeing of true nature into and of the light, above all challenges of the will
Revealing jubilation from the synchronisation of unconditional hearts, minds and souls
With time spent in meditation
We learn, that beneath closed eyes, stillness is how we connect the dots over and again
To see, I am, a universe,
How we unfold with love letting go
Absent of time and,
Releasing the light.

You are...

Unconditional personified
Infinite and finite
Stay open
Swim against the rapids as the listener and the witness
Centred and balanced, tread your waters and flow
Submerged in awareness loving within the self first
Giving but never giving in
Believing the way of being as jubilation and joy
Light, slow and whole
Be the sub sonic sonar whispering sentimental reflections into the blues
Through guided wisdom on a rift of vibrations vicariously evolving
Stay open, blooming and flowing
In the dew before the night falls and the constellations spell your sign
Be a perfect breath of contemplation for your dreams
A romantic moment, in its self
A poetic promise to the unknown
Deep in the magical
Swimming in the soliloquies of your sweet aura under a rapid sky, in human
Where the blues play rhythmic music of the heart with love
You are limitless
Unconditionally personified for victory

Solo blooming

Solo bloom like an eagle in flight
Wherever the sky, whatever the clouds pass
Through all scintillation of light
An evolution into purpose over change
Into vibrations and levels
Unto compassion and the sun season, soaring to fly
Flying to soar, through dreams of the open night
Mostly a solo flight
Hearts unfolding, rays igniting, soul fire in the rush of rain in every share,
Reigning over everything and again
Forward blooming with the power of visualisation
Then journaling into a blissful shapeless poem for the sound
Forming quavers and staves as I dance into the sky out of yesterdays
Gratitude for the new
Sipping on life's hip-hops ups and vibrations
Cocktails of rhythm and blues rhyme in season
Chimes and woodwind for meditation reasons,
Waves and focus through beats and breathing
Unfolding the oceans in self, solo blooming
Beneath stars into the night,
into messages of the day, into change
Letting pass a wonder wall of global questions for the cause of the journey
infinite energy beneath galaxies, I am awareness
Hearing the seasons different
Sleeping tight and dreaming different
Loving and fathering like the lessons of my ancestors changing through me
Promising dreams in the daylight and love in every action of hands and heart
Passing on these wings under a bipolar climate, a juxtaposition of sky and fate
An evolution change,
Cold snap season done,
Flying solo
Like an eagle in flight for my young
Into the sun.

As Love

Self solving,
Seeking yet never really without
Living and loving with faith, unfolding with grace in the lessons of the light
The next stage of the journey, deep diving for the grounding, lyrical meditation
Journals in the making for emotional intelligence with flow
Evolution with purpose
Unconditionally loving beneath stars pushing purpose in every sunrise
With inspiration in short bars of divine energies
In balance, bountiful and endless
Self solving with guidance and gratitude from within
As love...

A Message of the Day

Faiths understanding
An affirmation of weightless intervention in prayer
A solemn word,
A mantra if you will
words on the inside for balance,
For the witness and the wellness
Holding forward from within integrity,
Glowing directions for the morning with meaning
A thankful smile overflowing with gratitude for another
Hearts centred infinite,
Being the universe within,
Full and beating,
Shining energised with bliss
Falling with free wills parachute,
In love with self and the divine
Through breath of consciousness imploded into messages in the light
Visions of a sun full day and a season that smells like rebirth of the soil growing a victory
Being of peace, beholding a superpower
Beneath a superstructure embracing sensitivity
Allowing the silences to unfold guidance clear and,
Open to all possibilities and positivity
Grounded in strength
Underlined by a unity of love and light,
Arriving as abundance in the magic of an affirmation
A mantra if you will
In every message of the day

Fatherhood

The inner illuminations of compassion,
Layers
The multiverse of a deep thinking man from days before
Taught through circumstances of my father and my brothers.
A man to become man, all outward seeking balance with inward strength bestowed on me yet always brought to discipline, never learning truly to release and let go
Unfolding moments past and future beholding self in the present
In the new, is the now
A kaleidoscope of a man's cheerfulness and a boys upbringing to meet the measure of his faith
To raise a son in all my reflections
To shine the colour sun in every smile of my achievements
In light of all his differences to my experience, trusting his own to be his bliss and his journey to behold
Then to learn his growth, is a gradual lesson in letting go
No judgement
Just overflowing and overwhelming pouring
Of response'ability, maturity and mostly to love learning to love in the deep end
Applying working ethics and values, learning to release in my will, for his will
To succeed in self sharing self, shedding shelves to lift him higher,
The steady contemplation and illumination of compassion
Forward love and fatherhood, the openness to stand then show how to stand in the spiritual being of a man
Soul direction in it's own decisiveness and growth, Loving, respectfully
Beholding acceptance and grace in the face of rejection, forgiveness and freedom to just be
The sacrifice all in love for the inner wealth of your child's bliss
The smile full reflection of the sun in his smile
Seeking inward to hone in on the teacher, hoping to pass on these words through mindfulness methods of becoming a man, embracing sensitivity and emotional intelligence
Saving and showing love as a philosopher of compassion and self care
So little man can raise self

Being the Witness

Messages from your intuition are profound in healing
They whisper different and, request you feel before you listen, in stillness
Just being the witness
Silence breathes a direction into spaces of the body so tension meets its maker
Energetic stretches required for the release, so i'm teaching myself to yoga
To go through, beyond senses
I Persist, for I am not the body
I am spirit exercising breath through consciousness
The body is consciousness and I,
I am exercising will, so the universe opens paths in response to my release
Expelling light
In every stretch I witness, every breath I shine through truth
The only place I am, in self aligned, with hopes and shades of newness and openness,
Shapeless shadows enlightened and colours residing in oneness
Unfolding compassion, in touch with chakra's that requires only time and breath to shift
For through is the only rift,
The only growth becoming balance
The only content is peace, offering and ritual
A stability stance shaped like star beginnings,
Each day becoming into awareness.
From when time was first read by human,
Sat under a shooting kiss between sky and fire
No matter under the moon only movement, awareness and intuition exercising breath
While over standing consciousness in every stretch,
Meditating and witnessing the insight of a universe within
Only there, is where the dance can begin, were the poetry is written, the creativity lies witnessing new messages and new art taking resonance in the healing
Whispering different beneath the moon, a star of infinite signs, heart centred in uniqueness, unfolding love above all
In each day a profound reflection of soul passions and progression
A gift in human I am, holding ego to account to evolve this soul path
Sewing and stitching into reality, down for the journey, into the infinite inner sanctum so direction feels like flow
Stillness in the music and meditations of the day
So the longest dreams cannot be slept on but, written as it was before, over and again
Witnessing the stars arriving through crimson skys to calculate time
A projection perhaps from the soul work and past lives but,
The next stage of the journey always is, shaped in hopes and deep like ocean floors
grounded for the rebirth, witnessing the waves of the healing,
becoming into balance.

The Sun

A power shines through the window
Eyes sat still, awakening
Colours like a double sunrise over an ocean
Reminds my heart how the sun lifts us
Waves crash from calming music
Spells peace behind the eyes bright red in the sense of sight
Nurturing this nature into harmony with songs of gratitude
My conscious mind does dances in the tranquility of messages of the day and space between the insight to uplift and empower, to affirm self
While feeling my aura infinite seeking only sanctuary
Gifts of peace surrounded only by the now
Hand on heart seeing myself in the suns light for like and, like for like for the first time
I am a reflection of the universes ember, dreaming of a love in bliss that looks like myself
Like my body is extended beyond the day into the everlasting under a naked lunar
and its daytime while the night falls, and I am still, in meditation learning to wield space saved for later, the reflection of I am
Breath work and healing next to the heart within the poem and a message of the day from the sun
A power shining through a window of wisdom
Resembling the light
A reflection I am

Spirit Animal Search

Picture
The sun at the centre of your heart

Breathe in

say the word 'Spirit'

hold your breath for an 8 count

Now breathe out

say the word 'Warrior'....

Interruption....

When you do a search with your child to find out   'What is your spirit animal Dad?'

together we find out his is a hummingbird, which is a perfect match.

I find out that my own is a turtle

Of all the animals

Why not Jaguar, or Eagle, or panther....

back to meditation.....

Breathe in

say the word 'Spirit'

hold for an 8 count

Now breathe out

Raphael....

Blindingly Jazzing the Rays

While time passes through under a day,
Blue clear
Music sounds like nature
Sun sits in glimmer jazzing rays
Blindingly
Infinite
Keys of enlightened energy shining
On whomever is below
Possibilities overflow
Into strength and the approach of the beyond releasing the before
Honour bestowed by the light
A road laid before us
To show us
We are King's and Queens,
Warriors, and
Knights, before the sky turns stardust in our sight
While time passes time under a days
Clear blue waves of bliss
Spirits honouring self allowing change to pass through
Chasing inner wealth and leading with abundance
Each of us
A sound, shining like nature and, nature sounding like nurture
Sun sits in glimmer blindingly jazzing the rays
Enlightened energy shines through
To accentuate your light

Weightless in Freedom

Treasure and love moments in the now
Every small small molecule of awareness counts fruitful to your actions
Lead compassionately with your manifestations at the centre radiating love
The embrace of being, determined and open
Breathe in the power of yours, to be one with everything
Vibrate at your highest elevation with flow
Each day as an earth day and a council of wishes, engulfed in natures wonders
Weightless in freedom toward your dreams, moments accumulated of the now into special
Blissful knowings, that are shaped from your imperfections into power
Into beautiful vibes and prayers
Solidifying purpose of your wisdom
Exuberating existence and flow
Weightless in freedom
Prosperous and compassionate just the way you are

We are layers of consciousness embodying energy claiming emotion, clearing and harnessing flow.
Souls of love moving through ego to unfold and embrace Divinity's becoming, in the everlasting
now, Endlessly evolving through passions of life
Beginning with breath
Journeying through the sharing of self with many hearts
Beings of light, limitless in spiritual perspective and inner wealth

Karma

Karma is most time synonymous with good
With balance, restored justice and the prevailing of a wish
After heartache or struggles
A lesson learnt and displayed by release
A courage attained in reward from growth through trial
Karma can in most times signify the beginning of a new, an end to a cycle
A peace unfolded from the overwork into a bliss
The spiritual unlocking of rest after a win or transformation
For acting with the purest of hearts
There's always a twist in the story,
That impact, the trajectory and release but,
Most times it is all just on time with your path and perhaps not with another's
Divinely guided in belief that with the right time comes also the direction towards a new karma
A restored balance unfolding joys, recognition of strengthened will and,
A quiet spirit of equanimity, justice and growth
Toward something finer and kindred in essence.

Breathe and Flow

Using all your senses within, breathe, listen and let it flow
Write the moments of the mystical into life
Into jazz under a jaundice skyline
Forevermore move with your divine essence of poetic self
Investing on a daily for the mastery
Seeking, solving dimensions
Inward cultivating wisdom in a rhyme
Rhythm were you are in the healing, in the story
Ink blotted and swimming in wishes
Allowing time to pass through
Only to venture into forward and untested waters
To glow through visions of infinite deserving's and release
Then walk the path of abundance at the centre
Aligned as you always are,
Shadows unwrapped from the moon dust
A message of the day given away
From these unfolding rituals each day
For poetry leads the way
Soul passions the offering
Meditation the healing
The pen once key now fingertip on screen using all senses
No codes, no matrix, just this god given talent, defined and combined on this ancestors trail, sitting honouring space
Recognising the determination consciousness bestows on the righteous when practising grace in a bountiful balance of energy
Witnessing the abandonment of all senses
Breathe and flow.

Dimensional

We are,
Self dimensional supernovas of symmetry
Some times, the sum of epiphanies emphasising beauty, most times an anomaly to the untrained
An individualism of Divinely guided wisdom listening for the meaning
We are,
Matter in the moments powered by the breath
Dots in the pages written by the soul then birthed into life to unfold the story unsystematic
Scribbled into nature with a will of magic from the beginnings of our endless dimensions.
Each day a meditation of awareness, yet unaware the extent of our spiritual
Intuition blinking sky in every sight
Seeing everything as a lesson to harness flow
            Far beyond the capacity to comprehend evolution into purpose and intonations
Into healing, and messages of empowerment and affirmations
To will the ego toward soul path creativity.
            Beholding acceptance next to passion
              Showing beauty, full in every moment that is most times more than words
                              Can be
        Actionable, accountable, without expectation exciting to put into smiles
                            Into eye contact and joys
We are
Vibrations that speak louder, without symmetry, that jigsaws together, each of us a piece by peace.
A soul path pre-destine, written through ego, leading and learning the body over lifetimes for the journey, Journaling the past and destiny in the present
            Light warriors living on the land of the sun
Spiritually writing the ways through from within
            Divinely guided and dimensional never without

Being of Oneness

From within,
Your heart is set on compassion,
Changing over time through influence yet it is shapeless, boundless, poetic and unconditional
Over spilling beauty, vibrating Divine frequencies at one with the universe
Seeking endless mysteries and moments everlasting

Dial in on the self care and set yourself on higher purpose with passion,
Butterflying the colours of your heart into phoenix wings
Envelope the now and stick to your inner source,
Sealing love in every letter and fire on every word
Growing from reflection and focused in the presence
Re-birth into every moment out of oneness
Transforming and unravelling uniqueness of spirit
Setting your life force frequency on limitless
Excel with consistency and gratitude
Encompassing your infinite capabilities through ritual and reward
With the power of breath piecing together your peace

Becoming one with the seasons
A present in the present moments overlapping layers of consciousness through breath and sight
Leading with equanimity and balance,
One of awareness and grace at every glance of serenity in the simplicity of each moment
Inked with all that can be told
All that can be music and be the free as the wind to reach the stars
From breath through to consciousness of body and spirit
A present in the present being of oneness, aligned and set on higher purpose through passion

Path Building on Abundance

Manifestations in slow motion
Seeing everything as the sun synchronisation sets on optimisation and self preservation for Divine essence
Miracle frequency
Unfolding succinctly as the imperfection of beauty
A melody of vibrations on high
Lyrical meditation on fly
A series of moments enhancing focus
Path building a dance between the breath and sight
acknowledging the abundance within heart, mind, body and soul
Blooming a thoroughfare of unspoken dreams
Growing through emotion
In the everlasting now

Live through your gifts, your talents and your soul passions
Let creativity be your source and your guide
Seeing into the curves and the corners of what brings you instantaneous joy is the view of your abundance unfolding
Rewrite and free-write your present and live with a faith that
Breeds Jubilation

Parallel Lines

Open up you heart chakra
Elevate, align
Sit centred in wonderment communicating with the Divine
Realising, no two paths lead the same way, but we mirror and intertwine
Like travellers on parallel lines,
Multidimensional and overlapping
Only when grounded do we connect vibrations at synchronised destinations
From crown chakra to root,
Meet me at the sacral of your light
And together we can align
Through our solar systems
To the heart

Poetry and Self

Unfolding the vibrations of grace
Seeking and soaring to become the vision within
The falling and getting up,
Teaching the self newness in every pose
Calming and balancing between the absence of linear,
In each breath holding the waves between the land and the ocean floor in consciousness
All in the spirit of writing something new each day
Embodying inspiration for poetry and self,
An affirmation of meditations in each reflection, in every stretch
Cultivating wisdom into purpose evolution
Legacy and peace over everything
Taking time for the focus to resemble the winds direction
For the love within expelling the light through creativity
Connecting the dots to determination and direction
Claiming acceptance and will,
Unfolding poetry to vibrate higher,
For this soul fire passion to release and flow, toward prosperity

Prosper in Your Greatness

Over-standing manifestation and patience
A natural power of seeing into wishes we all hold,
Moments unfolding intuition and claiming inner wisdom
Rewriting and free-writing songs of yesteryears into grace and present moment blessings
Knowing that the future is only a best laid plan and the past is but a memory.
That in the everlasting now is where you prosper in your greatness
Cherishing experience and basking in peace for the work.

Let time be a moment of free waves between the still waters
Less current more flow, between energetic life lines
That allows you less drift more go
Vibrations embracing third eye inspiration and living for the meaning
More depth and open heart receiving
Giving from a place of balance
So your crown Is filled with compassion, on everything
While continuing to be grounded in your dreams and living Divinely guided
Sharing shapeless moments for the meaning
To grow and raise, to guide self and young into conscious bloom
With peace and prosperity in mind and action,
In wellbeing and safety, building with others healthily and spaciously
Nurturing the nature in the now
Where your inner wealth is abundance
Shining your light with honour, love, laughter and,
Trust in the process, so you prosper in your greatness

Go Within

Let compassion open your heart to the flow of unconditional love
Go within and embrace the essence of your being as love
Give unto self care
Sit, centred
Seek in the infinite self
For peace
For forward movement without expectation
For the freedom
For the learning to be
In oneness, with independence and togetherness
Free yourself into equanimity and grace,
In the infinite beauty of you
Equilibrium with all elements of love, wealth, health and success
Balance and let loose
For unconditional love is the language of the spirit, unambiguous in flow

Kindness is Key

Each of us
A light and a seed
Filled sublime
Luminous
In righteous kaleidoscopic wonders of progress
Each of us
An epitome of guidance and discernment
Unearthing kindness is key
Within, so without expectation
Unlocking the light for the seed of guidance
Illuminating progress unconditional
Enhancing the spirit and vibrations to be
Each of us
A vibration sublime in the dark and the light
Blissful and shapeless in acceptance of self
Submitting to evolution and purpose
Abundance and wealth
In each of us
Filled with wisdom and light
We are, a sunset ceremony kissing the morning and night

Being Free

                In the faithfulness of unpredictability and the vitality of life

                                          Lies in the giving and,

                            The compassionate nature in each of us

Living your dreams and your prayers as they are answered

Trusting in the Divine guidance and intuitive direction
                          Free being,

                                                  to become.

In Peace

It is with determination
In peace
That we see the consciousness in everything
Knowing and trusting in your truth
That anything can be achieved
That direction is a matter of sensitivity and strength
Feeling your way through and toward
For meaning over moment
Using all senses, believing in the power of breath
Immersing yourself into truth and wisdom of the dimensional self
Knowing the personality is shapeless and,
Exercising ego less as a healthy mechanism for the soul to push forward
To unfold curriculum on time toward destiny's path
With sincere intentions
It is, with determination we must lead from the knowing and trusting within
Not the fixing of what we perceive as broken but the accepting and sharing
The unconditional love of imperfections where practice makes progress
The beauty of transformations and spiritual openness,
It is, with all the above we must act with compassion and
Let determination be a reflection of the hearts path to the magic of success and peace

PEACE

Posture

"Perfect balance comes by listening with humility to the inner wisdom of your flesh and bones"
'Teach yourself to meditate' by Eric Harrison

Good posture in meditation
Is being rooted in the awareness of bones and energy
Coccyx communicating with the earth, and the spine, straight, like the bark of a tree
Being
Listening for the rebirth of spring or the call of autumn
For the communication of energy in the wind
For the seasons sparks throughout the nervous system
Being, for whatever blossoms, for the jaundice in the sunshine
Renewing into focus
Of one with the atmosphere and self
Having a profound respect for the breath
For wisdom of the body and,
The signals from within

Meditation of the day

Spiritually elevated
Source code meant for legacy
Centred in imperfection
For truth and direction
Consciousness seeking new dimensions
Affirmation and true vibration
A knowing
That in each of us, is a dream state awaiting to wake
Pushing the shadow toward a light
Reflections mirroring left and right
A determination to rewrite the pages into moments of the dots that feel like love
To uncover meaning in the blink of your third eye
Showing togetherness is oneness
Within I am
Unfolding ritual today, and in every tomorrow
For the deeper communication and offering of positive vibrations and openness
Mantras for the soul vibes to unleash passion
To over-stand balance, soundscapes are on peace for the inner journey
Spiritually sovereign recognising the source code meant for legacy
Centred in abundance and compassion
Evolving from a message of the day to a meditation of the day
Reflections of peace and wisdom spiritually elevated in every share

Elevate

                  From the heart centre

                                            From the light you are

                      Release

Into the ethereal,

                As the vibration you are

                                          As abundant individuation

              Higher self over everything

Soul passion into purpose

                     Elevate
            Compassion as your being

Uplifting empowerment
For the healing and over-standing
Elevate

                              Piecing together the journal for the journey
                                                      To turn pages

Into solidarity for the process
Into trust
I am
Within
The path,
We are,

          A meditation series, a kaleidoscope of light beneath galaxies,
                                  A piece of heaven on earth in each of us
                           Beautifully beating bountiful rhythms of love,
                Beholding reflections of togetherness
                        At the heart
                Centre yourself in creativity
                     Now Elevate

Your Story

Beauty is being an ever-changing transformation of peace and joy, practice makes progress of the work
As we are
A peace, that allows growth

Know you are the listener, the witness, a being of breath
The prepared, well rested, free writing the work of the unfolding

Slow

How it's supposed to be to reveal your passions, like an evolution of purpose
Centred
At the pace of the strength of your story

Tuning into Life Force

Tuning into the body's default method of measurement of life force
Of prana, the breath

           Igniting the filaments of soul passion and learning to calm the path,
To align chakras and enlarge the aura.
              To be the water in my last name swimming into the corners of all life's possibilities,
                       Flooding this light into the root chakra,
                       Feeling the earths core support and,
Encompass the capacity of a free flowing mindset that knows only awareness.

  Tuning into creativity to meet the source, the mastery of mystery and manifestation over the aspect of
                       time and the monopoly of inner wealth
                       Knowing thyself and how to hold and,
                Explore your power, your Divine essence
Holding the solar in you, the light of you the sun in every smile and,
balance beneath the heart
                Centred
                How you pour into the self constantly and simultaneously, live in the meaning
Of life force over time, breathing without thinking most times to keep the circulation of the hearts music
playing into life.
knowing forgiveness and compassion are a cycle of the unknown meeting the body for the first time,
that breath is the beginning and the restart
Filling and extending the aura
                          Aligning chakras and,
                          Putting energy into faith,
                        Meditation over everything

Tuning into the bodies default method of measurement of life force
Of prana, the breath

Walking with Kindness

Displace the old beats in time and out of time into kindness to yourself
In so, that the strong beats survive
So that the sound clash becomes weak and the heart grows with forgiveness
Sounds of silence absolute in freedom and softness of rhythm through motion and breath
Free to write with the spirit and set free the nervous systems
Through nature and nurture, entirely into peace and jubilation
Into silence and symbology of old language new talk, energies combined
New magic and consciousness in your walk
Removing the concept of man's time revealing Divine setting, now walk
In absolute heart and new music of kindness
Music of truth and authenticity

ABUNDANCE

Being of gratitude

Just being
Faithful
Hopeful, for the journey journalling the syllables and connotations
Leaning in to the scenery of consciousness and self
A wisdom forefront cultivated in the morning messages of the day
Nurtured and untested, syncopated with nature through breath
Checking in on the bountiful levels of divinity within
That sounds like music, like poetry
Where each of us are just as exemplary as the other in reflection of every note and quaver
every hair and freckle, every complexion complete
A magnitude of excellence in creation
each and every one of us
The essence of awareness and acceptance
Recognising right paths from what was left paved by creativity and drive
A resonance
Being of I am
Of love and grace
Is how your light reflects your beauty
When just being
Of gratitude

Creativity and Grace

Allow yourself to be graceful
Know that your divine journey is timeless and,
You are ready and capable, just as you are,
You are where you're supposed to be
Trust that in self your soul plan is inevitable and, your dreams are limitless
Begin to flow creatively as a being of love and endless joy

Your creativity is life giving back to life.

The Art of Will

We are born of love and prosperity
Of life and longevity over and again, paths moulded and set in,
Soul passions playing out amongst the reveal of clarity
We are not here to seek it, but merely be it
Walk with it as we are infinite awareness, eternal in spirit and one with the universe,
We are longevity within and, loves message of the day
Beings of prosperity, within what makes this existence harmonious and tumultuous,
Endless with possibility of soul passions playing out amongst the revelations of clarity
Free to be the art of will
One with serenity through peace of mind
One with being love in all its working shapeless shade of prosperity
A peace and flow of conscious blessings blooming, breathing
Learning to be
Evolving purpose, endlessly,
In love and of love unfolding
releasing light and clarity of soul passions self and all that is the art of will
Endless awareness and vibrations of life
Sharing all your uniqueness with your will to receive,
Abundance revealed as a constant present self, unwrapping and letting go the conditioning
Uplifting soul passions playing out the magical frequencies of miracles and life
Learning to be
The art of will

Clearing

Learning to clear in meditation
Focusing on the breath, and for every thought or emotion that arises naming it,
Claiming the feeling and sitting with it
Then clearing it, letting it pass and back to the breath and,
Expanding on silence,
Knowing that the emotions are the language of the soul and,
The silence is not the goal, but the witnessing,
The listening
The claiming and the clearing,
The naming and the letting go,
The expanse of breath into the spaces between thought and emotion, allowing soul awareness to connect you to the body and release,
So that your light can shine through

Everything you do, is the unfolding of your souls written path pushing ego spiritually beyond the shadow into the healthy heights of achieving your infinite purpose.
Receptivity and,
Self compassion is your superpower, your love language of simplicity and grace.

Embrace the sound of silence and the music of everything
For maximum exposure to your gifts

Divinity Unseen

Moving platforms under a new moon
Shining a light on connection
A power miss-taught under the suns light of purpose
An independent level of consciousness, I am
We are of the shadows nature
One with the body and visible in every light
Shapeless in the sharing
Through wordplay and the caring
All slowly unfolding into endless reflections of oneness and being
Seeing and beholding the differences and imperfections
Honouring light, nature and the mystical
Through the irreplaceable levels of sky from the ground up
Connecting hearts centred in the light and the night
While platforms create a new and,
Consciousness resembles the silence in everything
We are dimensions under a new moon
Moving platforms for a vista of Divinity
Written but unseen

Reflections of Bliss

Spreading wisdom through the body at the clearing of emotion and words in the sounds of silence
Sitting in stillness,
Sometimes movement is required for the nervous system to settle
Or the chakras to align and the blockages to be open
So all that is derived and syncopated is breath and body
Inexplicably of consciousness and bliss in every awakening
Like forever in an unchanging horizon
Lit by the suns kiss of love and kindness within
In the dusk of a crimson view, I meditate with the moon
At the clearing of fears and settling in stillness, poetry and the self meets word of mouth
Holding red sky's behind closed eyes and unspoken words beneath tongues dancing jovial into the blues at the back of ones mind
The calming music provokes visualisation so the words become a story into a melody and,
The ambience in the newness floating on every depth of awareness within
Spirit levelled and intoxicated with bliss, clear of the unspoken or emotion of past fears released into light and replenished into wisdom were silence through the body meets peace
it is the sound of a pause between inhalation and free release that illuminates the path,
Cultivating wisdom to turn stillness into clarity and expansion into light
So Divinity sublime appears in reflections of bliss

Infinitely Journeying

Be a vibration that reflects the bountiful beginnings of your love unfolding
Infinitely deserving of love returning
Revealing peace personified by awareness
Infinitely journeying as Divinity's light shining through the self as oneness

Be the measures of acceptance
Between the sounds of nature and the soul, accepting how you find the in-between, as love

The vibrations of all encompassing, unfolding transformations, absent of time
Absorbing the real, as awareness of all that is accepting of the now

Be the values within and without judgement
Applying grace and humbleness with the capacity to offer self true peace and poetry
The romance of self care and true excitement of growth and sharing unconditionally
Breathing out success with every force of natures sounds of life, living full without forcing
Embracing the measure of will and acceptance
Growing in love and awareness of spiritual wealth
A conscious vibration sublime,
Like all that is of acceptance,
I am the bountiful beginnings of love unfolding
Infinitely journeying

For Jericho

You are free to be, effortlessly
The outcome of your will

A seed of clarity in every awoken moment
Free to summon in every wish your dreams into this reality
Standing over every challenge, triumphant and grown
You are whatever you will to be,
You are free to be, effortlessly

With a firm grip on courage, and the freedom of humility and vulnerability
Your will, my son, is to be, pure of heart and free as love

As you rhyme and rhythm the beauty of your existence and,
Live as a vibration of blessings,
The music of my heart
Be compassion that sounds like the blues in all directions of your dreams
Your will is your awareness of will, to be, effortlessly free as you are

To be brave and courageous in all your becoming
When you're working the songs of your truth,
Your spirit will light up the hearts of many and, your dreams will be the clarity in every breath before your eyes

Before you move and when you move the outcome is you,
Always of love
gigantic over everything, standing over freedom,
Pure of heart as you flow and grow in every song
Effortlessly becoming to be who you are
Free in your will

Synchronicity

When synchronicity hits,
Manifestation, is like seeing into the curves of a new beginning in every breath
Preservation is key
Faith is the bliss of awareness,
That in every moment is meaning like waves between the waters still,
Ocean currents and depth, drinking symphonies into life that allows everything of your will into worth
To connect all feeling of body and breath with your peace like water to the earth
Infused with vibrations that fill the soul
Actions into foresight through kindness into plan,
Unfolding the goal
Unto love, health and nurture with honour,
With laughter and trust
In Divine timing showings us we are light through everything
Bright as anything, shapeless like water
When synchronicity hits
It sometimes reflects like rain, mixed with shards of sunshine
Before a kaleidoscope of rays
Then colours the ground to show the way

There is only now in the message

A journey of hearts, aligned in array
Beginnings blooming,
All lights from within
With intentions of grace and intonations of blessings
Infinite possibilities, without expectation
Spirits of will
Free,
                                      Being,
                              Full and centred
                              In equilibrium
                              Bound for peace

There is only now in the message
New in each day
Journaling for the heart through vibrations sublime to clear the waves
All light from within
A will of clarity and oneness
In every meditation of the day

Being the work of the present, propel yourself beyond measure
Be weightless
Be a molecular movement of conscious concentration within and freedom without
Be a strengthened will, realising the gift of kindness
Be the work and, the present
Witness being the listener and the guidance

MOTD-LIFE

2022 Copyright (c) Joseph E L Baruwa BSc
All rights reserved

Printed in the United Kingdom

This book may not be recreated or reproduced in written, verbal, electronic, mechanical or any other form, by any means without permission of the writer.

Cover art and all written work, produced and published By Joseph E L Baruwa BSc DipBSOM
Meditation teacher
#MOTDLife.

Teaching yourself the art of will through Yoga is trusting your awareness of body and becoming freedom and having the courage to let go